A LOOK AT EARTH'S ROCKS

WHAT ARE SEDIMENTARY ROCKS?

BY FRANCES NAGLE

Gareth Stevens PUBLISHING

CRASHCOURSE

Please visit our website, www.garethstevens.com. For a free color catalog of all our high-quality books, call toll free 1-800-542-2595 or fax 1-877-542-2596.

Library of Congress Cataloging-in-Publication Data

Names: Nagle, Frances, 1959- author.
Title: What are sedimentary rocks? / Frances Nagle.
Description: New York : Gareth Stevens Publishing, [2018] | Series: A look at Earth's rocks | Includes bibliographical references and index.
Identifiers: LCCN 2016037137| ISBN 9781482462418 (pbk. book) | ISBN 9781482462425 (6 pack) | ISBN 9781482462401 (library bound book)
Subjects: LCSH: Sedimentary rocks--Juvenile literature. | Geology--Juvenile literature.
Classification: LCC QE471 .N34 2018 | DDC 552.5--dc23
LC record available at https://lccn.loc.gov/2016037137

First Edition

Published in 2018 by
Gareth Stevens Publishing
111 East 14th Street, Suite 349
New York, NY 10003

Designer: Samantha DeMartin
Editor: Kristen Nelson

Photo credits: Series background winnond/Shutterstock.com; caption box Edhar Shvets/Shutterstock.com; cover, p. 1 mangojuicy/Shutterstock.com; p. 5 Hans Strand/Getty Images; p. 7 Rhonda R/Shutterstock.com; p. 9 nayladen/Shutterstock.com; p. 11 AJP/Shutterstock.com; p. 13 Betty Shelton/Shutterstock.com; p. 15 Ivan Smuk/Shutterstock.com; pp. 19, 30 Sementer/Shutterstock.com; p. 21 Parmna/Shutterstock.com; p. 23 BarryTuck/Shutterstock.com; p. 25 (bottom) Fletcher & Baylis/Getty Images; p. 25 (top) corlaffra/Shutterstock.com; p. 27 (inset) anat chant/Shutterstock.com; p. 27 (main) Krizek Vaclav/Shutterstock.com; p. 29 Styve Reineck/Shutterstock.com.

Printed in the United States of America

CPSIA compliance information: Batch #CS17GS: For further information contact Gareth Stevens, New York, New York at 1-800-542-2595.

CONTENTS

Earth's Surface	4
Weathering	6
Erosion	10
Pressing Down	14
Kinds of Rock	18
The Strata	22
Fossils and Fuels	26
How Do Clastic Sedimentary Rocks Form?	30
Glossary	31
For More Information	32
Index	32

Words in the glossary appear in **bold** type the first time they are used in the text.

EARTH'S SURFACE

About 75 percent of Earth's land surface is made up of sedimentary rock. Sedimentary rock forms when sediment is **compacted** over a long time. Sediment is small pieces of matter, such as stones and sand.

MAKE THE GRADE

Sedimentary rock is only 1 percent of the rock that makes up Earth! Our planet is mostly made of the other two kinds of rock, **metamorphic rock** and **igneous rock**.

WEATHERING

Sedimentary rock can be found all over the world. Its formation starts with weathering, or the breakdown of rock by wind and water. As wind and water move over rock, they slowly wear away pieces of it.

MAKE THE GRADE

Physical weathering creates sediment such as sand, soil, and clay.

Water and other matter can cause **chemical** weathering when added to rocks. They might make the rock softer or cause it to break down. Gases, such as oxygen and carbon dioxide, can have this effect, too.

MAKE THE GRADE

Weathering is often shown as the first step in the rock cycle, which is the model scientists use to show how rock forms, breaks down, and re-forms over time.

EROSION

Once created, sediment often moves! It might be blown away by wind, carried by water, or pulled down a mountain or hill by **gravity**. When sediment moves from where it started, it's called erosion.

MAKE THE GRADE

The number one cause of erosion today, by far, is people!

As sediment is created and moves, the pieces of rock often hit each other. Some pieces become smaller. They become smooth and round from bumping and sliding against other sediment. Sometimes, this movement sorts sediment by size or type of rock.

MAKE THE GRADE

A common place to find sediment is at the bottom of a body of water.

PRESSING DOWN

Sediment finally settles in a new place. Other matter builds up on top of the sediment, pressing on it. Over time, the sediment is buried. As **pressure** increases, the sediment is compacted.

MAKE THE GRADE

As matter builds up on top of sediment, people and animals may walk on it. Water may flow over it. This all adds to the pressure that helps form sedimentary rock.

As the sediment is compacted, water flows into the open spaces of the rock. **Minerals** that are **dissolved** in the water fill the open spaces. This helps the sediment bind together into sedimentary rock.

MAKE THE GRADE

As buried sediment is binding together, more sediment may be settling on top of it, adding pressure and also starting its own rock formation.

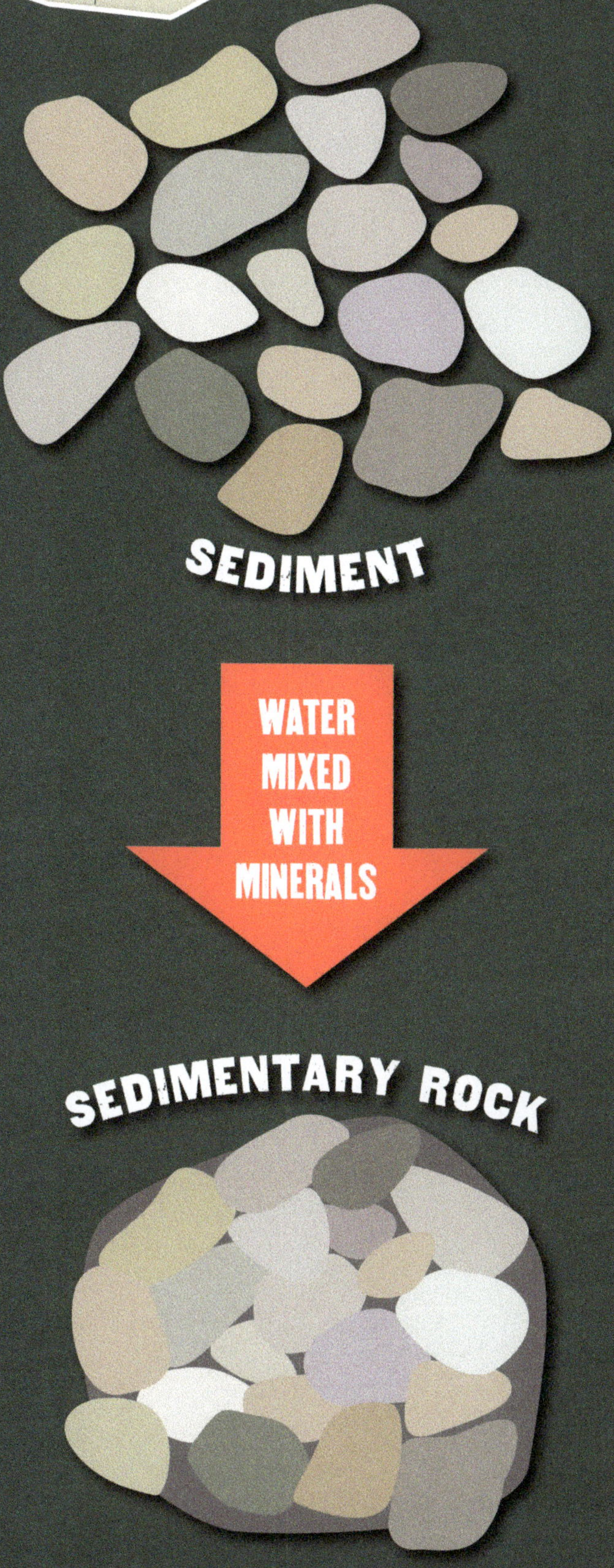
SEDIMENT
WATER MIXED WITH MINERALS
SEDIMENTARY ROCK

KINDS OF ROCK

There are two main kinds of sedimentary rock. Clastic sedimentary rock forms from the sediment produced by weathering. It's the most common sedimentary rock and sometimes has shells, pebbles, or other large matter in it.

MAKE THE GRADE

All the big and small rocks and bits of matter that make up clastic sedimentary rock are called clasts.

Nonclastic, or organic, sedimentary rock can form from the buildup of minerals in a drying area of the ocean. The remains of living things, such as the tiny shells of sea creatures or dead plant matter, can also become nonclastic sedimentary rock.

MAKE THE GRADE

Though the sediment is different, nonclastic sedimentary rock goes through the same process of **lithification** as clastic sedimentary rock.

THE STRATA

Sedimentary rock sometimes looks like it has stripes! These **layers** are called strata. They're often different colors and thicknesses, depending on where the rock's sediment came from, how much settled there, and what minerals are in it.

MAKE THE GRADE

Strata at the bottom of sedimentary rock are older than those at the top.

Stratification is the formation of strata. Many strata are nearly **horizontal**. Others aren't straight and show the direction wind, water, or gravity moved the sediment as it formed rock. Some strata have clasts ordered by size, from largest to smallest!

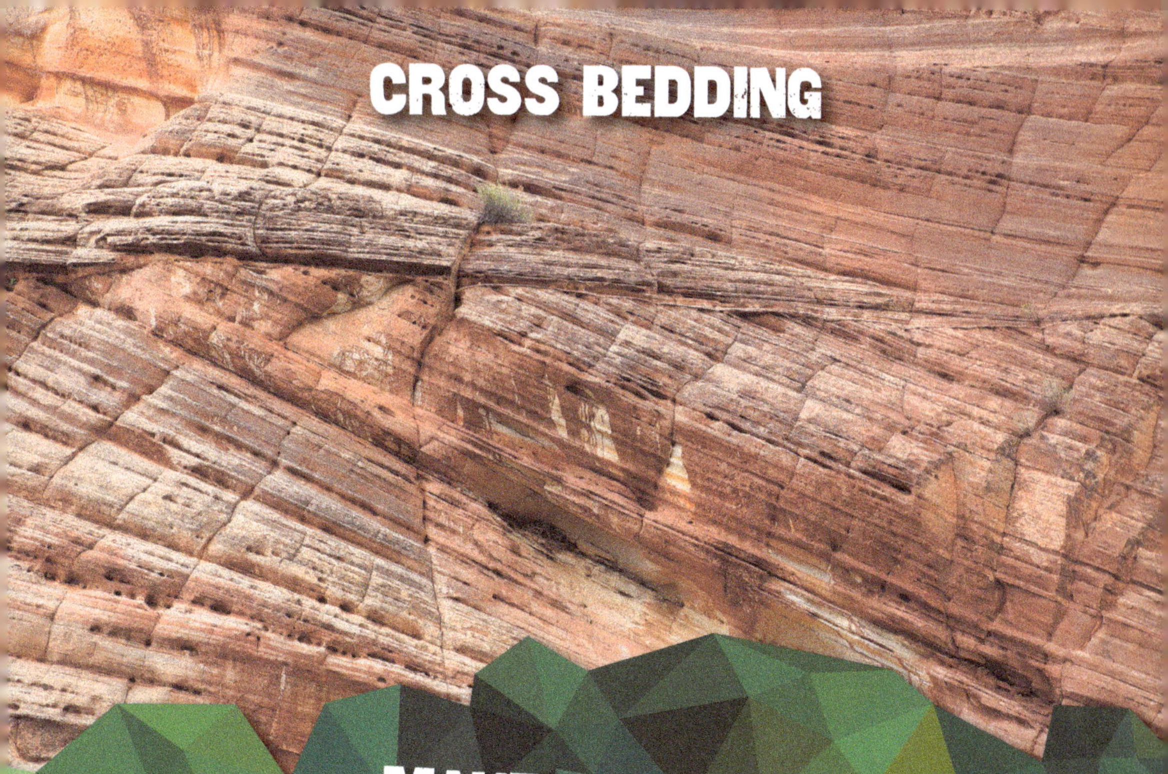

CROSS BEDDING

MAKE THE GRADE

Stratification is also called bedding.

GRADED BEDDING

FOSSILS AND FUELS

Sedimentary rock formation has produced important **natural resources** called fossil fuels. Organic sedimentary rock that formed from compacted plant matter becomes peat. With enough time, heat, and pressure, peat becomes coal! Both coal and peat can be used for power and heat.

MAKE THE GRADE

Fossil fuels are any matter made on Earth that can be used to make energy, such as oil and natural gas.

Sedimentary rocks are studied to learn about Earth's history. That's because they contain fossils! Where they're found in a rock's strata can help scientists find out what life was like on Earth millions of years ago!

MAKE THE GRADE

Fossils are the hardened remains or marks of past plants and animals.

HOW DO CLASTIC SEDIMENTARY ROCKS FORM?

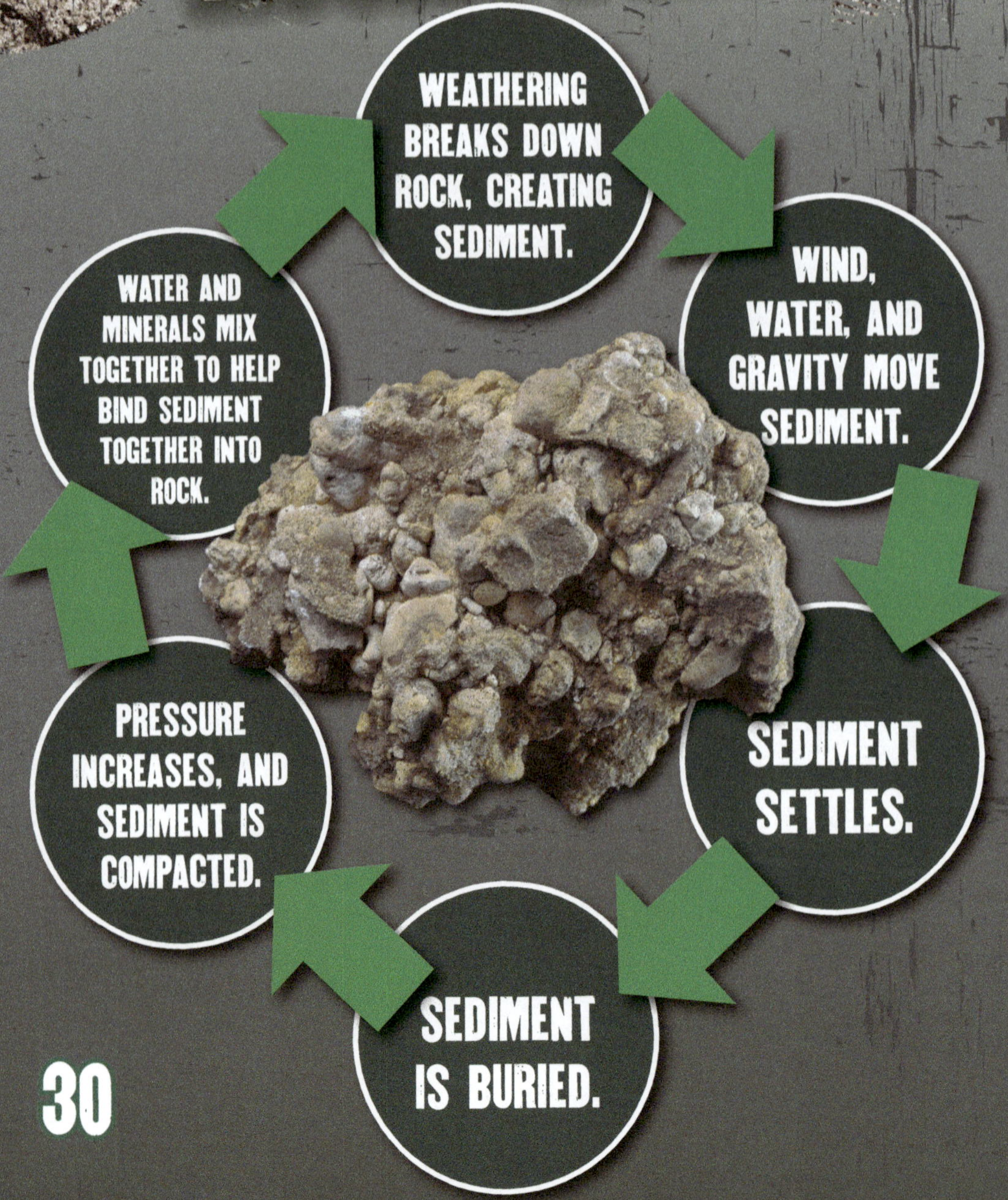

GLOSSARY

chemical: having to do with matter that can be mixed with other matter to cause changes

compact: to force closer together

dissolve: to mix completely into a liquid

gravity: the force that pulls objects toward Earth's center

horizontal: level with the line that seems to form where the earth meets the sky

igneous rock: the rock that forms when hot, liquid rock from within Earth rises and cools

layer: one thickness of something lying over or under another

lithification: the process by which sediment becomes rock

metamorphic rock: rock that has been changed by temperature, pressure, or other natural forces

mineral: matter in the ground that forms rocks

natural resource: something in nature that can be used by people

physical: having to do with matter

pressure: the application of force

FOR MORE INFORMATION

BOOKS

Hansen, Grace. *Rocks*. Minneapolis, MN: ABDO Kids, 2016.

Lindeen, Mary. *Investigating the Rock Cycle*. Minneapolis, MN: Lerner Publications, 2016.

WEBSITES

Geography4Kids.com
geography4kids.com/files/earth_rocktypes.html
Read about all the kinds of rocks and how they form.

The Rock Cycle
eschooltoday.com/rocks/the-rock-cycle.html
Check out an illustration showing the rock cycle.

Publisher's note to educators and parents: Our editors have carefully reviewed these websites to ensure that they are suitable for students. Many websites change frequently, however, and we cannot guarantee that a site's future contents will continue to meet our high standards of quality and educational value. Be advised that students should be closely supervised whenever they access the Internet.

INDEX

clastic sedimentary rock 18, 19, 20, 30
coal 26
erosion 10
fossil fuels 26, 27
fossils 28
gravity 10, 24, 30
lithification 20
minerals 16, 20, 22, 30
organic sedimentary rock 20, 26
peat 26
pressure 14, 15, 16, 26, 30
rock cycle 9
strata 22, 23, 24, 28
stratification 24, 25
water 6, 8, 10, 15, 16, 24, 30
weathering 6, 8, 9, 18, 30
wind 6, 10, 24, 30